You and Me

Your Fair Share

Denise M. Jordan

Heinemann Library
Chicago, Illinois

Customer Service 888-454-2279
Visit our website at www.heinemannlibrary.com

Designed by Sue Emerson, Heinemann Library; Page layout by Que-Net Media™
Printed and bound in China by South China Printing Company Limited
Photo research by Janet Lankford Moran

08 07 06 05 04
10 9 8 7 6 5 4 3 2 1

Library of Congress Cataloging-in-Publication Data
Jordan, Denise.
   Your fair share / Denise M. Jordan.
         p. cm. – (You and me)
Summary: Explains how to share pencils, toys, and chores.
   ISBN 1-4034-4409-9 (HC), 1-4034-4415-3 (Pbk.)
   1. Sharing in children--Juvenile literature. [1. Sharing.] I. Title.
   BF723.S428J67 2003
   177'.7–dc22

                                   2003012816

Acknowledgments
The author and publishers are grateful to the following for permission to reproduce copyright material:
p. 4 Visuals Unlimited; p. 5 Nancy Sheehan/PhotoEdit Inc.; pp. 6, 7, 8, 9, 10, 11, 12, 13, 22, 24 Que-Net/Heinemann Library; pp. 14, 15, 16, 17, 18, 19 Warling Studios/Heinemann Library; pp. 20, 21 Robert Lifson/Heinemann Library; p. 23 (T-B) Felicia Martinez/PhotoEdit Inc., Myrleen Ferguson Cate/PhotoEdit Inc.; Que-Net/Heinemann Library; back cover (R) Felicia Martinez/PhotoEdit Inc.

Cover photograph by Norbert Schaefer/Corbis

Special thanks to our advisory panel for their help in the preparation of this book:

Alice Bethke, Library Consultant
Palo Alto, CA

Eileen Day, Preschool Teacher
Chicago, IL

Kathleen Gilbert,
Second Grade Teacher
Round Rock, TX

Sandra Gilbert,
Library Media Specialist
Fiest Elementary School
Houston, TX

Jan Gobeille,
Kindergarten Teacher
Garfield Elementary
Oakland, CA

Angela Leeper,
Educational Consultant
Wake Forest, NC

Some words are shown in bold, **like this.**
You can find them in the picture glossary on page 23.

Contents

What Is a Fair Share?

Sharing means some for you and some for me.

Fair shares are **equal** groups.

You can find many ways to share.

You can share in many places.

How Can You Share Chores at Home?

You can clean your plate after dinner.

Your sister can clean her plate after dinner.

You both have one chore to do.

That is a fair share of the chores.

How Can You Share with Your Sister?

You can share your toys with your sister.

You have four toy cars.

You let your sister play with two cars.

That is a fair share of toy cars.

How Can You Share with Neighbors?

You picked six **tomatoes** in your **garden.**

You keep three tomatoes.

You give your neighbor
three tomatoes.

That is a fair share of tomatoes.

How Can You Share with Your Community?

Your neighbor is collecting books for the **community center**.

You have two of the same book.

You keep one book for yourself.

You give one book to the community center.

That is a fair share of the books.

How Can You Share at School?

You can share with your classmate at school.

You have ten crayons.

You give your classmate five crayons.

That is a fair share of crayons.

How Can You Share with Your Friend?

You can share with your friend.

You have two dolls.

You give your friend one doll.

That is a fair share of dolls.

How Can You Share on the Playground?

You can share turns jumping rope.

You have a turn.

Then, you let someone else have a turn.

That is a fair share of turns.

How Can You Do Your Fair Share on Clean-Up Day?

On clean-up day, everyone helps.

Everyone can help clean up
the park.

You can pick up a piece of trash.

If everyone does what they can,
that will be a fair share of
the work.

Quiz

There are five slices of pizza.

There are five children.

What is a fair share?

Look for the answer on page 24.

Picture Glossary

 **community center**
pages 12, 13

 **equal**
page 4

 **garden**
page 10

 **tomatoes**
pages 10, 11

Note to Parents and Teachers

This book offers children the opportunity to explore the concept of sorting a group of objects into smaller equal groups while sharing with others. An understanding of sorting lays the groundwork for the concepts of division and fractions. Children are presented with varying numbers of items or tasks and shown how they can equally share those items or tasks with another person. This book can serve as a springboard for math activities in the context of everyday life. For example, at snack time you might present an even number of cookies or pieces of fruit and use "math talk" to guide children in identifying the concept of fair shares and equal groups.

Index

Answer to quiz on page 22

One slice of pizza is a fair share.

24

ml

1/05